They came from the hills. Rooted in Scot-Irish and German traditions, men and women brought their music to Nashville. But not to Nashville alone. They went wherever there was a radio station or a recording studio. They went to Bristol and to Kingsport, to Memphis and to Lexington. The Cajuns went to Baton Rouge and to Shreveport, while others went to Tulsa and to Kansas City.

Singer-songwriters migrated from their farms and ranches into nearby cities with the hope of singing on the radio and being recorded. They brought with them their hillbilly, Cajun, German, and western swing traditions.

In the beginning, Nashville was one of many destinations for these men and women. With the advent of WSM's Grand Ole Opry going out to all America, Nashville soon was the top prize.

They sang about themselves and their lives. They sang about loving and about dying. They sang about their hopes and their faith. They sang about betrayal. And so, country music was born.

NASH

VILLE

THE PILGRIMS OF GUITAR TOWN

PHOTOGRAPHY BY

MICHEL ARNAUD

TEXT & STORIES BY ROBERT HICKS

DESIGN BY JOEL AVIROM

STEWART, TABORI & CHANG
NEW YORK

*Published in 2000 by
Stewart, Tabori & Chang
A division of U.S. Media Holdings, Inc.
115 West 18th Street
New York, NY 10011*

*Distributed in Canada by
General Publishing Company Ltd.
30 Lesmill Road
Don Mills, Ontario, Canada M3B 2T6*

Library of Congress Cataloging-in-Publication Data

Arnaud, Michel.
    Nashville : the pilgrims of guitar town /
photography by Michel Arnaud ; text & stories
by Robert Hicks ; design by Joel Avirom.
        p. cm.
    ISBN 1-55670-989-7
    1. Country musicians—Tennessee—
Nashville—Portraits. I. Hicks, Robert. II. Title.

ML87 .A77 2000
781.642'092'276855—dc21   99-057641

*Edited by Marisa Bulzone and Julie Ho
Graphic Production by Pamela Schechter*

*Design Assistants:
Jason Snyder and Meghan Day Healey*

*The text of this book was composed in
Granjon Italic, captions were composed
in American Gothic.*

*Printed and bound in Hong Kong
by C&C Offset*

*10 9 8 7 6 5 4 3 2 1
First Printing*

To Liz Tilberis

CONT

ENTS

Hopes & Dreams 2

Acknowledgments

We would like to acknowledge all who allowed us into their lives to photograph them, and their families and managers who opened doors and gave us access. You all make up the host of individuals who made this possible. This book is the fruit of your labor and your kindness to strangers. Hopefully, you know who you are and what you've done for us, for there are far too many of you to name.

Yet among all of you, it would be amiss if we did not single out those who gave special support for this book: our publisher, Leslie Stoker, whose enthusiasm made this dream come true; Marisa Bulzone, our editor, whose guidance helped us through the project with a great sense of ease; Hazel Smith, the legendary publicist, and Beth Nielson Chapman, singer-songwriter, who went above and beyond in their assistance— to you and all the others involved our deepest gratitude and thanks.

Preface

The first time I stepped into a bar on Lower Broadway in downtown Nashville, I found it neither remarkable nor glamorous. There was a small stage in the corner, close to the entrance of the bar, where someone was singing and playing his guitar. It was about two o'clock in the afternoon and the bar was almost empty, only a couple of people were there drinking, and they paid little attention to the singer.

There was nothing very impressive about this scene; it was rather an image of a down-and-out Nashville. It certainly wasn't how I visualized the famous Nashville I had heard so much about in France.

I asked about the musician performing on stage, and I was told that he played four hours at a time and just for tips—occasionally a drink might be offered by the house or from someone in the "audience." I looked around again at the empty saloon, and it really hit me—this guy wasn't in that bar for the money, he was there for a break into the world of country music. He was chasing his dream to succeed in the town that could allow those dreams to come true.

When Robert Hicks drove me around town on a guided tour of sorts, I realized why Nashville was so special, why people first came and why they still come—bringing their hopes and their dreams.

I thought of the Pilgrims who first came to America, and the waves of immigrants since then who have come in search of their dreams, whatever they may be. To a European like myself, Nashville is the perfect symbol of the American Dream. It is a uniquely American phenomenon that remains fascinating to outsiders. I had to tell the story of Nashville; that became my dream.

Now that dream has come true and I have come to love Nashville. My only regret is that my visits will not be as frequent. I already miss you, Nashville.

—MICHEL ARNAUD
NEW YORK, NOVEMBER 1999

INTRODUCTION

I first encountered country music over twenty-five years ago as I stood shivering in the side alley of the old Ryman Auditorium one December night. Earlier in the evening I had met a questionable girl in a questionable bar who had come to Nashville to be a country music star. I had never met anyone who wanted to be a country star before that night. If the truth be known, I'm not sure I knew anyone before that night who even *liked* country music. I liked her—at least I did that night in that bar. She was amazed at my ignorance of Dolly, Loretta, and Tammy, and I was fascinated by her fascination with them as I listened to her reel off their biographical details.

Several hours later there we were in the alley that served as the backstage for the *Grand Ole Opry* at the old Ryman. Originally built as a gospel tabernacle by a born-again river boat captain, this brick and stone pile had been transformed several times over the years: from revival meeting hall to community cultural center to the fifth and most famous home of WSM radio's *Grand Ole Opry*.

Like any backstage, there were goings and comings as acts moved on and off the stage into the alley then into Tootsie's Orchid Lounge beyond. The closer I got to the door up the steps from the alley, the warmer I became, owing to the Ryman's amazingly efficient heating system that was pouring warmth out into that December night.

I was awed by all that surrounded me. Everywhere I looked there were country music stars. Admittedly I wasn't able to identify any of them, but whoever they were, they sure dressed the part. I knew at that moment I was encountering a new and fascinating world.

These folks not only dressed unlike anyone I had ever met before, but they acted unlike anyone I had ever been around.

I wasn't from Nashville, but had come here to go to college. I spent my first couple of years here in the society of people who took pride in their disdain for country music. I remember my introduction to a fellow student whose family was among the handful of families that owned the insurance company that owned the radio station that owned the *Grand Ole Opry*. I remember him summing up *his* Nashville's vision of the *Grand Ole Opry*: "We own it, but we never go there." Most of my friends were embarrassed by the title "Music City, USA." I mean, what kind of education could you be getting in "The Home of America's Music?" And while we're at it, who had died and made country music America's music anyway?

What about rock 'n roll, or the blues, or jazz? Anything would have been preferable to us than country music. So here we were, my fellow students and I, going to college in a town whose name was synonymous with a form of music that appalled us.

Until that December night, the only country songs I knew were the first verse of "Your Cheating Heart" plus all the verses and chorus to "The Ballad of Jed Clampett," better known to me then as *The Beverly Hillbillies* theme song. Yet for some reason I found myself drawn to those "hillbilly" musicians who were laughing and smoking and shivering in the alley with me that night.

They openly expressed themselves in a way that I had never seen adults do. Nothing seemed hidden in their world—neither their rhinestones nor their feelings.

One couple stood at the edge of the crowd slapping and shoving each other all the while screaming accusations and counteraccusations of alleged infidelities. The spectacle of this drama seemed to amuse some of the onlookers while others seemed oblivious. Perhaps they had witnessed this scene too many times before. This all came to an end only when a young man came barreling down the steps of the Ryman to tell the woman that she was "on in five minutes." At this announcement the fighting stopped and her enemy-lover began to touch up her ruined makeup.

What a far cry all this seemed from my world, where the image of propriety was everything. My mother's response to family discord, when she couldn't quickly end it, was to shut the windows lest a passerby realize that harmony did not reign universally within. Where I came from, we neither spoke nor sang of cheating or betrayal. Such fears needed to be kept to oneself. But in that alley the folks were loud and they were happy—even when they weren't. Even in their costume they seemed authentic to me.

Once I finally got inside the door I was overwhelmed by Captain Ryman's work of penance—the tabernacle that he had built to celebrate his liberation from a life of sin. Unlike the costumes in the alley and on the stage before me, the cavernous sanctuary was neither opulent nor gaudy. Puritanical in its severity, the room recalled its early years as a Fundamentalist revival hall. Even though it was December, I can still close my eyes and see the flash of hundreds of cardboard fans as the audience vainly tried to keep cool while watching the seemingly never-ending string of performers. They must have heated the place with those old heaters they used to heat high school gyms when I was growing up, for they sure cranked it out.

After that night, I never met up with my guide again. I don't think that dream of hers ever came true. At least to my knowledge it didn't. Yet somehow I was never to be the same. The next weekend I was back in that alley: this time I came to listen to the folks arguing and loving in the alley and the folks singing about arguing and loving up on the stage.

Now, when I sit in the Bluebird Cafe and look out the window at the grocery store parking lot across the street and squint my eyes, I don't see an empty parking lot; I see orange groves. For Nashville remains even at the turn of this century what Hollywood must have been about the time the talkies first appeared. And like Hollywood in the late 1920s—half city, half orange grove—Nashville remains a mythical place where pilgrims come to make their dreams come true. This book is about the pilgrims who have come to the city truckers call Guitar Town. A few have seen their dreams come true. Some have not. Most never will. Yet for all those who fail in their quests—some staying and redefining their dreams, some never giving them up, some going back home—there are those who are making it. One way or the other, there is something quite extraordinary about men and women driven by their passions and dreams, and willing to risk everything to achieve them.

A couple of years ago Michel Arnaud came to Nashville to photograph my cabin for a shelter magazine. I had been prepared by the magazine for a rather difficult, demanding, and well known fashion photographer from Paris. Nothing could have been further from the truth except, of course, that Michel Arnaud *is* a well known fashion photographer and he *is* from Paris. If he is demanding, it is of his own work. If truth be known, Michel may be one of the least difficult Parisians around.

By the end of the second day of shooting, I had him down on Lower Broadway walking the streets, bar hopping, and listening to music. I tried to explain that to me Nashville was and is about hopes and dreams. Whether fulfilled or lost along the way, those dreams remain our story. Michel loved what he saw and what he heard—and he got it. As the night wore on he began to talk about how extraordinary the people looked. This was coming from a Frenchman who lives in New York City? I began to wonder if *I* got it. Yet as he pointed out those who were so familiar to me, I began to look at them anew and remember that it was these dream-filled pilgrims who first captured my heart.

That night we discussed the project that has now become this book. We realized that neither of us had any interest in chronicling the twenty top-grossing artists of the Nashville music industry. Nor were we interested in producing another photographic encyclopedia of the same. What we were and remain drawn to are the dreams of Nashville's dreamers. We wanted to tell a story in pictures and words of both those who come here and chance everything and those who are just passing through.

So, in telling this story we have drawn from both the city's fixtures, like the Opry's Porter Wagoner and the Bluebird's Amy Kurland, and those who are only passing through, like Jules Shear or Mark Bryan. As Guy Clark said, "Few of us are really from Nashville and none of us stay. Oh, we may die here, but none of us stay." In a similar way, because Michel and I were interested in the dreamers of dreams, we had to tell the stories of Alan Jackson, Earl Scruggs, and Dolly Parton. It also would be a very incomplete story without Buddy and Julie Miller, Todd Snider, and John Hiatt.

None of us can dispute any longer what I once so easily denied: Nashville is what it is today because of country music. Yet that said, to limit the city to only our country heritage is to limit it indeed, no matter how rich that heritage remains. To understand Nashville one can neither deny the depth of that heritage nor define Nashville by the Saturday night Opry roster. Nashville remains both Pam Tillis and John Kay, Naomi Judd and Lambchop, Chet Atkins and Billy Cox, Kostas and Leon Russell. While such an understanding may confuse those in either camp who would prefer a simpler answer, it has remained our guiding vision throughout this project.

Since that first visit to Nashville, Michel has come back many times. The first few trips we mostly discussed the parameters of the project. It seemed to me that if a French fashion photographer of Michel's renown could look at a rustic American interior with a fresh eye, surely he could bring that same freshness to a photographic study of Guitar Town. If our goal was not to photograph everyone, who would we photograph to best tell Nashville's story?

Along the way we listened to a lot of music, attended a lot of "guitar pulls," and showed up at a lot of "rounds." Michel came to understand what Bonnie Raitt meant when she said that there was "more talent in an hour in Nashville than there was in a month in L.A." Likewise, he has sat through some pretty insufferable, talent-free moments.

Some twenty-five years ago, about the same time I was having my first encounter with country music, Robert Altman told the story of dreams and hopes in his masterpiece *Nashville*. When the film came out, the old guard that prided itself in its disdain of country music and the very music industry it disdained temporarily joined forces in a united hue and cry against the film. One could not go to a drinks party in Belle Meade or hang out in one of the many bars near Music Row without hearing someone begin to rage that *Nashville* was not the Nashville they knew.

Somehow Altman had pulled one over on us and had made us the butt of a joke we didn't understand. We seemed unable to transcend our personal fears of being laughed at long enough to ask ourselves if he might have some larger issue in mind. While the film critics in New York saw the film as a metaphor of our nation's lost direction and cynicism after the years of Vietnam and Watergate, we in Nashville wondered why Altman's Sunday worship scenes didn't include a Church of Christ, and why he couldn't have filmed more of our lovely houses, or Cheekwood, or the Steeplechase. As America tried to put the puzzle of its meaning back together, Altman's characters floundered about without hope. We didn't understand.

In the years since the Altman's film crew left, Nashville didn't sit still. In the late 1970s, country music seemed to hit bottom after making a rather bad marriage with Urban Cowboy pop. Yet just when its critics and doomsayers had all but managed to bury it, country music seemed to find its roots and be born again. The early- and mid-1980s brought about a true renaissance for the Nashville's music industry. Through the likes of Randy Travis, George Strait,

Steve Earle, and so many more a new generation was introduced to country music. Alan Jackson, Garth Brooks, Reba McEntire, Billy Ray Cyrus, and a host of others played key roles in taking Nashville's music further than anyone had ever dreamed possible. Success breeds success, or so they say, and for a while Guitar Town became Boom Town. Unfortunately, when you continue to make copies of copies the image becomes fainter and fainter. As the century turns, Nashville stands at a crossroads again.

If the music all seems to sound pretty much the same on country radio these days, that's because it is. The radio programmers of country radio have all but destroyed the format as they continue to narrow the standards for what is acceptable to them for the airwaves. They don't want songs about mother or prison or heaven or hell. They want uptempo, positive love songs. The narrowness of their formula rules out songs like "He Stopped Loving Her Today," and eventually it rules out George Jones, Dolly Parton, and Johnny Cash. Steve Earle, the Mavericks, and Lucinda Williams will have to find other formats.

Nashville is faced with many issues as it enters this new century, yet through the ups and downs, it remains the mecca of dreamers. The flood of the music industry from southern California to Nashville may come to a stop if our sales remain in a slump, but no slump will stop the dreamers. They will continue to come. Some will be buried here, others will only pass through, but they will come. As long as we can squint our eyes and see orange groves where others see only parking lots, Nashville will remain that spot on the map where all things are possible.

This is our story, this is our song. As with Altman's *Nashville*, most everyone who picks up this book will have a better idea of who should or shouldn't have been included. This Nashville will not be their Nashville. They will be right. As Michel and I worked on this book, we grew to believe, like Altman, that although it is certainly about Nashville, it is really about something much bigger.

For Michel, that night on Lower Broadway opened musical windows within him that usually close down in all of us over the years. He who had chased after the Rolling Stones as a up-and-coming photographer was now chasing after Connie Smith and Jack Ingram and Beth Nielson Chapman. As he bought this vision of Nashville as a symbol of all our hopes, he began to re-evaluate his place in the world. Perhaps Nashville is a paradigm for a greater archetype: America. In telling the story of these pilgrims to Nashville maybe we are telling the story of the American experience.

At this time in his career, Michel could have continued to live comfortably as a French citizen residing in America. Yet as we worked on this book over the last couple of years, this no longer seemed adequate. It wasn't enough merely to observe and photograph the dreamers, for he like all of us has his own dreams. Near the end of our last shoot, Michel became an American citizen. No longer simply the observer, he has cast his lot with the rest of us. This story is now his story, too.

—ROBERT HICKS
NASHVILLE, NOVEMBER 1999

GUITAR PULL

Every night, all over Nashville, men and women get together to "pull" a guitar around some room. Born in a time when few folks owned their own guitar, this tradition began as an informal circle where a guitar was passed, or pulled, around, to all the players. As casual as a few friends who gather on a porch after work to sing songs they grew up with, or a couple of would-be songwriters in a kitchen who share their latest attempts, guitar pulls abound in this Guitar Town.

This particular pull has been gathering every couple of months for about nine years out at this two-hundred-year-old log cabin in the hills south of Nashville. While there are both blue-collar pulls and celebrity pulls, this group has always sought a mix. You never know what you'll get when John Kay is sitting next to a house painter, Beth Nielson Chapman next to a tractor trailer driver, and Mary Chapin Carpenter next to a waitress.

Kevin Welch once said of such a pull, "This sort of community is the very reason I came to Nashville in the first place. Even before I had ever heard of a guitar pull, I always thought that this is what folks did up here."

THE PILGRIMS OF GUITAR TOWN

HOPES & DREAMS

I SING
ONLY FOR
TIPS !
THANK YOU

ne way or the other, there is something quite extraordinary about men and women driven by their passions and dreams, something out of the ordinary about those who chance everything.

MATT KING
HENDERSONVILLE, NORTH CAROLINA
SINGER/SONGWRITER

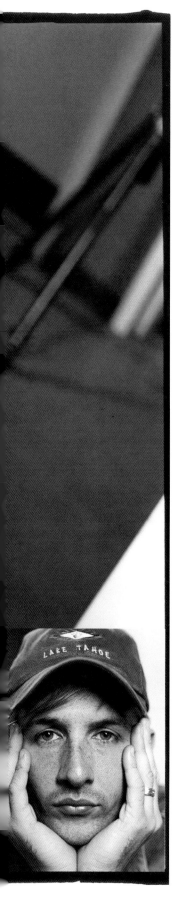

8

ALLISON MOORER
Frankville, Alabama
Singer/Songwriter

ERNEST ALOYSIUS CHAPMAN, THE THIRD
NASHVILLE, TENNESEE
MUSICIAN/POLITICAL ACTIVIST/SKATEBOARDER

RIGHT
HEIDI HIGGINS
ALTAMONT, ILLINOIS
SINGER/SONGWRITER

TROY JOHNSON

KATY, TEXAS
SINGER/SONGWRITER

A couple of years ago Alex Torrez called me up and wanted to make an appointment to give me a CD of demos of a young singer-songwriter he had signed over at Sony Music. Alex can't ever just send you something, he always has to make an appointment to give it to you in person. I told Alex my plate was full and there really wasn't anything I could do for anyone beyond what I was already doing. Alex was at my office within an hour.

We listened to two or three songs by a young artist named Troy Johnson. Troy had grown up in Katy, Texas, and had come to Nashville to go to college. More likely, Troy had come to Nashville to get into music; school was just a way to please his parents. Now Alex was out working that dream of Troy's.

It wasn't hard to be impressed with what I heard, but my plate was still full when Alex left my office that afternoon. Over the next year I had occasion to hear those songs again, usually by accident when I was trying to find some other CD while driving.

About a year after Alex's first visit, he was back in my office talking to me about Troy. Along the way Troy has had some success as a country songwriter, but his whole approach to his own career is more Eric Clapton and John Hiatt than it is Clay Walker. You hear his songs and you don't know where he'll be in ten years, but you want to be around then to see where he lands.

When I finally met Troy, I knew I was in the presence of someone who is driven by vision and ambition. I'm not talking about some kind of blinding egomania, but a sense of self that transcends his youth.

STEVE EMLEY
CLEVELAND, OHIO
SONGWRITER/TOUR MANAGER

BRETT & BRAD WARREN
TAMPA, FLORIDA
SINGERS/SONGWRITERS/BROTHERS

EVAN LOWENSTEIN

ATLANTA, GEORGIA

SINGER/SONGWRITER/IDENTICAL TWIN

GEORGIA MIDDLEMAN
SAN ANTONIO, TEXAS
SINGER/SONGWRITER

If each story is different, it may be equally true to say that each story remains the same. Georgia Middleman came to Nashville by way of Texas and California and, like so many before her, waited tables while trying to find a publishing deal which might lead to a record deal, etc. Despite her patience and good cheer, it seemed for a while that Georgia was destined to be a legend among waitresses.

At long last, however, she secured the elusive publishing deal and shortly thereafter signed a record deal. Georgia could finally entertain the thought of parting with her waitress uniforms. Of course to do so would break the cardinal rule for rising stars: never give up your day gig.

After all, doesn't legend have it that Tammy Wynette kept renewing her Alabama beauticians license for years, fearful that her music career would end?

ABE MANUEL
MAMAU, LOUISIANA
COONASS/MUSICIAN

Abe is a coonass from southern Louisiana. He's proud of it. He started coming to Nashville over forty years ago hoping to make it in country music. When nothing came about, Abe finally went home to Louisiana.

When two of his children moved to Nashville to try their hand at the business, Abe and the rest of the family ended back up in Tennessee.

He took over running his son's rural grocery store in Milton. Along the way he began to cook Cajun meals in the back of the store. Now he has a full-flung restaurant and folks drive hundreds of miles to Milton.

On Friday and Saturday nights, Abe and his family sing and play for the folks. Abe finally has the career he always wanted. It's just a little later than when he had hoped for.

MIKE KELLEY
PEKIN, ILLINOIS
SINGER/SONGWRITER

NATE BARRETT
BOSTON, MASSACHUSETTS
GUITAR PRODIGY

Unlike most of the rest who come here, the ten to fourteen who make up Lambchop really do want to keep their day jobs while making music professionally. With an ambitious touring schedule that has included European venues, this eclectic gathering of part-time musicians tries to maintain a balance between their commitment to their day lives and their nighttime music careers. While most of the band lives in and around Nashville, one member still flies in from Chicago, and another drives up from Athens, Georgia to perform.

They're the first to say that they are not out to change the world musically or make a killing in the business. They just wanted to find a way to sustain their dual lives and make it work. So far, so good.

WARNING!
THIS AREA PROTECTED
BY
NEIGHBORHOOD WATCH!
Join Hands With The Badge

LAMBCHOP

SINGERS/SONGWRITERS
INCLUDING

ALEX MCMANUS, ATHENS, GEORGIA, RESTAURANT WORKER/CONSTRUCTION
JOHN DELWORTH, ROCHESTER, INDIANA, MAILROOM CLERK
JONATHAN MAIX, NASHVILLE, TENNESEE, MANAGING EDITOR OF *NASHVILLE SCENE*
DENNIS CRONIN, VIRGINIA BEACH, VIRGINIA, WEBSITE DESIGNER/STUDIO TECHNICIAN
MARK NEVERS, NOWHERE, USA, RECORDING ENGINEER
DEANNA VARAGORA, CHICAGO, ILLINOIS, RECORD DISTRIBUTOR
KURT WAGNER, NASHVILLE, TENNESEE, WOOD FLOOR INSTALLER
PAUL BURCH, WASHINGTON, D.C., WORKS IN ENGLISH DEPARTMENT AT VANDERBILT UNIVERSITY
MARC TROVILLION, MEMPHIS, TENNESSEE, REMODELING CARPENTER
ALLEN LOWERY, NASHVILLE, TENNESEE, CITY OF BRENTWOOD WATER DEPARTMENT
SCOTT CHASE, CORNING, NEW YORK, REMODELING CARPENTER
PAUL NIEHAUS, ST. LOUIS, MISSOURI, CIRCULATION MANAGER OF *NASHVILLE SCENE*

JUMP, LITTLE CHILDREN
ROCK BAND
MATTHEW BIVINS
JAY CLIFFORD
EVAN BIVINS
WARD WILLIAMS
FROM
WINSTON-SALEM, NORTH CAROLINA
JONATHAN GRAY
FROM
DURHAM, NORTH CAROLINA

WHEN DREAMS COME TRUE

In a town where you often sense that every waitperson has come to make a big splash in the country music pond, the odds of success would appear to be pretty slim. In reality they probably are—and always will be. Yet, for all those who finally pack it in and go back home, there are also those all around us who are fulfilling those very dreams. In turn, it's these legendary successes that continue to draw each new generation of pilgrims.

Those who do succeed come in all makes and models. If they have anything in common with one another, it may only be the gift to persevere in the face of all those who have told them they couldn't make it.

KENT AGEE
RICHMOND, VIRGINIA
ARTIST/SONGWRITER

ANGELO
PELHAM, NEW YORK
SONGWRITER/PRODUCER

BETH NIELSON CHAPMAN
AIR FORCE BASES EVERYWHERE
ARTIST/SONGWRITER

Beth and her husband Ernest moved to Nashville from Alabama so she could pursue a career as a singer-songwriter. That path has taken some odd twists along the way. Ernest died of cancer in 1994, leaving Beth and their son, Ernest, to rebuild their lives without him. Her talent, combined with the openness with which she has always lived and the deep respect so many within the Nashville community had for Ernest, made her story our story, her loss our loss.

Beth approaches life with a sense of wide-eyed amazement that seems to have no end. A songwriter respected by her peers throughout the world, she seems immune to the jadedness that often comes with fame.

Her fans have included Bonnie Raitt, Elton John, the Prince of Wales, Bette Midler, and Mother Teresa. Her songs seem to be cut by everyone. Elton John summed up Beth's writing when he praised her song "Sand and Water" before he would perform it in concert, saying it was a song he wished he had written.

And so life for Beth goes on. She writes songs we wish we had written while she struggles with her new life, a teenage son, and the ongoing insanity we call the music industry.

KENNY CHESNEY
LUTTRELL, TENNESSEE
ARTIST

40

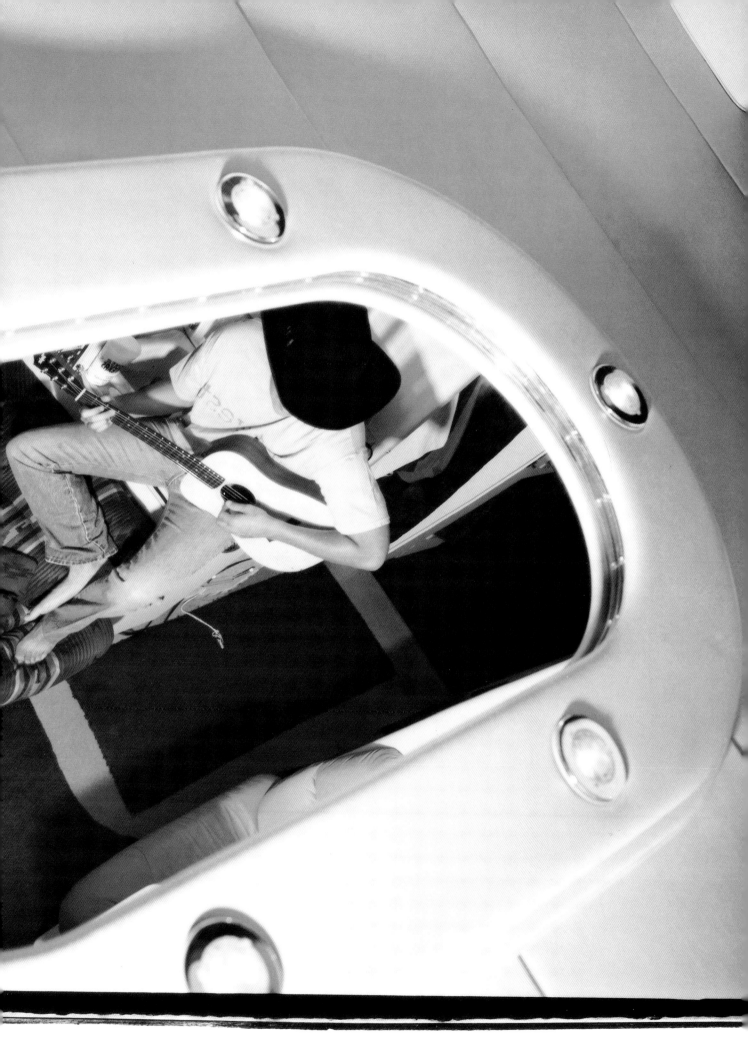

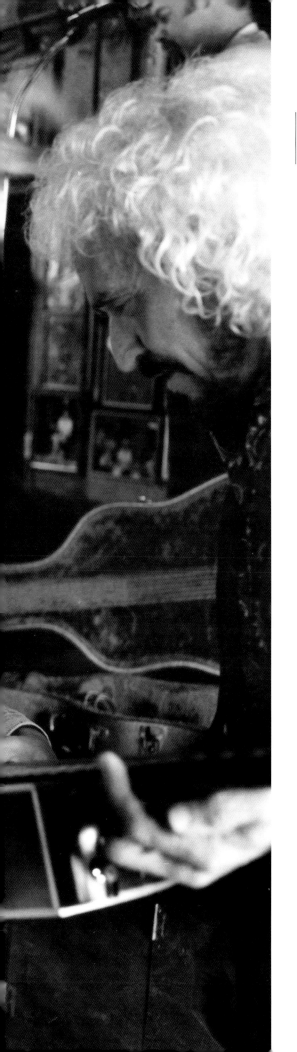

GEORGE DUCAS
HOUSTON, TEXAS
SINGER/SONGWRITER

Born the son of an oil company engineer in Texas City, Texas, George Ducas divided his growing up years between San Diego and Houston. By his mid-teens, he could near perfectly imitate his music hero, Willie Nelson. Already a veteran songwriter by then, his first composition (at the wise age of twelve) he titled "Women and Whiskey, Mighty Risky."

One of only a small minority who ever came to Nashville to actually go to Vanderbilt only to end up in music, George did a year of international banking after graduating. As it turned out, he spent most of that year playing into the morning hours in local bars, then nodding off at work the next day. During that year as a banker, George realized that his child-hood passions—music, the Padres, and the Chargers, not necessarily in that order—remained his true pas-sions. Figuring he had a better chance in the music business than he did of making either of the other teams, George left banking to pursue the dream.

It will never be like playing for the Padres or the Chargers, but Willie would be the first to tell him that even the best of lives will never be perfect.

JACK INGRAM
THE WOODLANDS, TEXAS
TROUBADOUR

When I told Guy Clark that Jack Ingram said that his goal in life is to be Guy Clark when he grows up, Guy told me to tell Jack to raise his standards a bit. Actually, what he told me is unprintable, but I think I'm relaying the spirit, if not the exact words of Guy's thoughts on the matter.

Following in the tradition of such Texas troubadours as Guy, Townes Van Zandt, Ray Wylie Hubbard, and Jerry Jeff Walker, Jack Ingram is introducing another generation of Texans, via the college club circuit, to songs about rowdy living.

Yet, for all his rowdy airs, Jack takes the job of songwriter and entertainer seriously. As Devil-may-care as he comes across onstage, he displays a commitment to his vision that's unyielding in focus.

Unlike many of his contemporaries, this vision is not multi-focused. Jack is the first to say that he doesn't harbor ambitions to cross over into some other field like acting. What he wants to do is get really good at being Guy Clark and figures a goal of such magnitude will take the rest of his life.

45

JIM LAUDERDALE
THE CAROLINAS
SINGER/SONGWRITER

TO
JIM LAUDERDALE
ONE OF MY BEST 'COOL' FRIENDS!
YOUR PAL,
BUCK OWENS
AUGUST 12, 1998

DAVE "BUCKET" COLWELL
BERKHAMSTED, ENGLAND
SONGWRITER/GUITARIST
BAD COMPANY

BILL MILLER
First Nation Visionary from
The Stockbridge-Munsee (Mohican) Tribe
in Northern Wisconsin
Painter/Musician/Songwriter/Visionary

Of all who have come to Nashville with their vision and dreams, whether it be from East Prussia or the British Isles, none seem to have traveled deeper than Bill Miller. They may have traveled further, but never deeper.

A child of the Stockbridge-Munsee Reservation in Wisconsin, and Mohican-rooted in both his ancestors' ways and his own coming of age in the 1960s, Bill has spent his life blending the Indian flute with Neil Young, the Ghost Dance with Jimi Hendrix, God with Bob Dylan.

A painter, a disciple of God, a songwriter, a musician, Bill Miller came to Nashville to pursue not only a career, but credibility. His struggle is forever with him as he tries to bring all the pieces of his heritage together and make them one.

Like so many growing up in France after World War II, Michel was enamored with the American West in book and cinema. The very possibility of photographing Bill delighted Michel.

If America is, indeed, the story of our pilgrimage, then are not those who crossed the Bering Strait our first pilgrims? Michel and I were taken aback by his humility and gentleness in a business that neither fosters nor rewards either. Possessing a deep spirituality without being "spiritual," Bill radiates his passion for the God of creativity. A faithful son who has become brave.

MARK BRYAN
GATHERSBURG, MARYLAND
ARTIST

Mark Bryan may be one of the nicest guys in the music industry today. For that matter, Mark may be one of the nicest guys on Earth today. As a member of Hootie and the Blowfish, Mark has known a great deal of professional success over the last few years. Yet he seems immune to its dark side. In his company, it's always about you and your wellbeing. He is a genuine fan of his music heroes and an encourager of everyone else. Between life on the road with the band and his family in South Carolina, there is scarce time to hang in Nashville these days. But every once and awhile, Mark shows up to write with and be in the circle of his fellow dreamers once again.

DERYL DODD
DALLAS, TEXAS
SINGER/SONGWRITER

MATT HENDRIX
NASHVILLE, TENNESEE
SINGER/SONGWRITER/BARTENDER

TODD SNIDER
PORTLAND, OREGON
SINGER/SONGWRITER

GORDON KENNEDY
NASHVILLE, TENNESSEE
SONGWRITER/PRODUCER

KOSTAS
SALONIKA, GREECE & BILLINGS, MONTANA
SONGWRITER/ARTIST

JIM SHERRADEN
SALINA, KANSAS
SONGWRITER/PRINTER/GRAPHIC ARTIST

On any given day in Nashville it can seem like everyone you meet is a songwriter, yet songwriting is the primary source of income for only a handful of them. Jim Sherraden came to Nashville to be a songwriter. Songwriting has never proven to be his primary source of income, either.

Unlike most of the rest of his fellows, Jim is neither a waiter or carpenter, nor is he in real estate. Jim runs Hatch Show Print, the oldest letterpress print shop in the country. Hatch has printed posters for Bill Monroe and for Elvis, too. B.B. King, the Rolling Stones, and Bruce Springsteen have all called on their services.

They print the old-fashioned way down there at their shop on Lower Broadway. They use the old presses. When a part of one of their presses breaks down, they may end up searching out print shops in India or Southeast Asia for used parts, as none of these parts are manufactured any more.

Some years ago Jim began to experiment with a new technique. He combined old wood and linoleum cuts with movable-type printing, painting free hand over the resulting print. His art is good. Hatch was already an extraordinary place before Jim came there; under his management it has become even better.

There is an earnestness and passion to what Jim does. He prints and paints like a songwriter should.

RAUL MALO
MIAMI, FLORIDA
VOCALIST/SONGWRITER
THE MAVERICKS

ROBERT ELLIS ORRALL
Boston, Massachusetts
Artist/Songwriter/Producer

BELA FLECK
New York, New York
Banjo Player

64

KEVIN WELCH
OKLAHOMA CITY, OKLAHOMA
ARTIST/SONGWRITER/RECORD MOGUL

*By the time Kevin Welch was seven years old
he had already lived in seventy different places.
When his family decided to settle down in
Oklahoma City, his father drove Kevin several
miles from their new home to Route 66. He
showed Kevin the highway and said, "Son,
don't worry; if you go left this road leads to Los
Angeles and if you go right you'll be in Chicago."*

*Sure enough, by the time Kevin turned
seventeen, he had hit the road to play in honky-
tonks across America. In the late 1970s, Kevin
came to Nashville to learn to write songs with
a somewhat off-center vision of what the country
music industry should be. He made several
attempts over the years to conform, but fortu-
nately always came to his senses before he had
done any permanent damage to his vision.*

*When he realized he couldn't change the
industry, Kevin and some of his comrades rein-
vented their own version of the industry in the
form of Dead Reckoning Records. I doubt any
of them would claim it's been a piece of chess
pie, but they have survived and even flourished
artistically. They have produced quality music,
enriched our community, and given Nashville
an alternative vision of the way things can be.
Along the way Kevin became a fine songwriter.*

*He's here in Nashville for now, but it's good
to know that the road is always there, just like
his father said.*

BR-549

FROM LEFT
GARY BENNETT, COUGAR, WASHINGTON
DON HERRON, MOUNDSVILLE, WEST VIRGINIA
SMILIN' JAY MCDOWELL, WEST LAFAYETTE, INDIANA
CHUCK MEAD, LAWRENCE, KANSAS
"HAWK" SHAW WILSON, TOPEKA, KANSAS
MUSICIANS/SONGWRITERS

The guys who make up BR-549 met while playing in neighboring bars along Lower Broadway, catching each other's shows during their respective breaks. Their formation of BR-549—a critically-acclaimed hillbilly band—was one of those legendary events in Music City history.

As word spread of the group's mix of lightheartedness and rooted country music, the band became a major influence in the reimaging of the bar scene on the streets near the river. Playing almost nightly in their early days at Robert's Western World, just three doors down from the famed Tootsie's, the band built a following big enough to panic a fire marshal. Their popularity grew to the point that at times the sidewalk in front of Robert's looked more like a club scene out of New York than a hillbilly bar in Nashville, except, of course, few folks were wearing black. BR-549 mixed traditional country-western cover tunes with their humorous originals—and they made it all look like fun.

Music critics wrote about them, the foreign press wrote about them, travel writers wrote about them, even the New York Times *wrote about them. For a couple of years, no trip to Nashville was complete without the obligatory hang at Robert's. For the umpteenth time, hillbilly music was cool again.*

The critics and purveyors of coolness liked to speculate in those days whether BR-549 would ever be able to translate the phenomenon beyond Lower Broadway and on to record. When the record deal finally did come, everyone had an opinion whether BR-549 would sink or swim. As it turned out, the band did swim. With subsequent success, BR-549's venue has grown from Lower Broadway to the world.

JONELL MOSSER
LOUISVILLE, KENTUCKY
VOCALIST

In a town where music is everywhere, Jonell can pack a club for several nights in any given week on a regular basis.

When she is on stage, there is a rare union of song and voice and heart. Jonell describes her style as soul music. She says she likes to flatter herself by thinking she's attempting to follow in the steps of Otis Redding. Well maybe Otis Redding with a little Al Green, David Crosby, Little Feat, and Gladys Knight thrown in. With a recklessness that is more akin to Townes Van Zandt than most of the women who should be her role models, Jonell's style is never safe. Coming from a business that often seems to be constructed of nothing more than hype and spin, superlatives become meaningless. Yet when Don Was described Jonell as "one of the greatest singers in the world," he may have been guilty of understatement.

MATRACA BERG
NASHVILLE, TENNESSEE
SINGER/SONGWRITER
JEFF HANNA
ASPEN, COLORADO
FOUNDING MEMBER OF
THE NITTY GRITTY DIRT BAND

SUZY BOGGUSS
ALEDO, ILLINOIS
SINGER/SONGWRITER

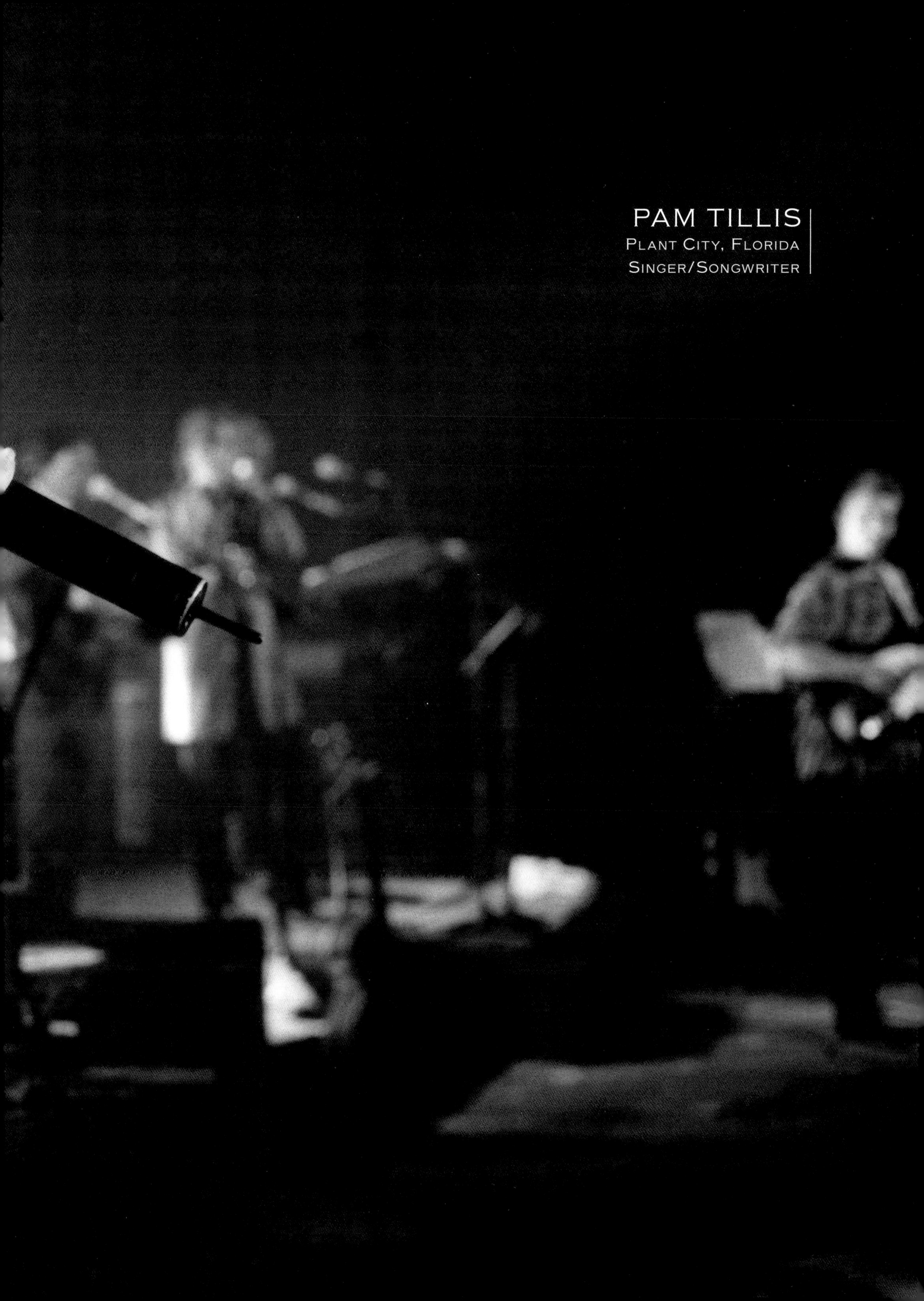

PAM TILLIS
Plant City, Florida
Singer/Songwriter

FRED KOLLER
HOMEWOOD, ILLINOIS
SONGWRITER

HARRY STINSON
NASHVILLE, TENNESEE
DRUMMER/RECORD MOGUL/
SINGER/SONGWRITER

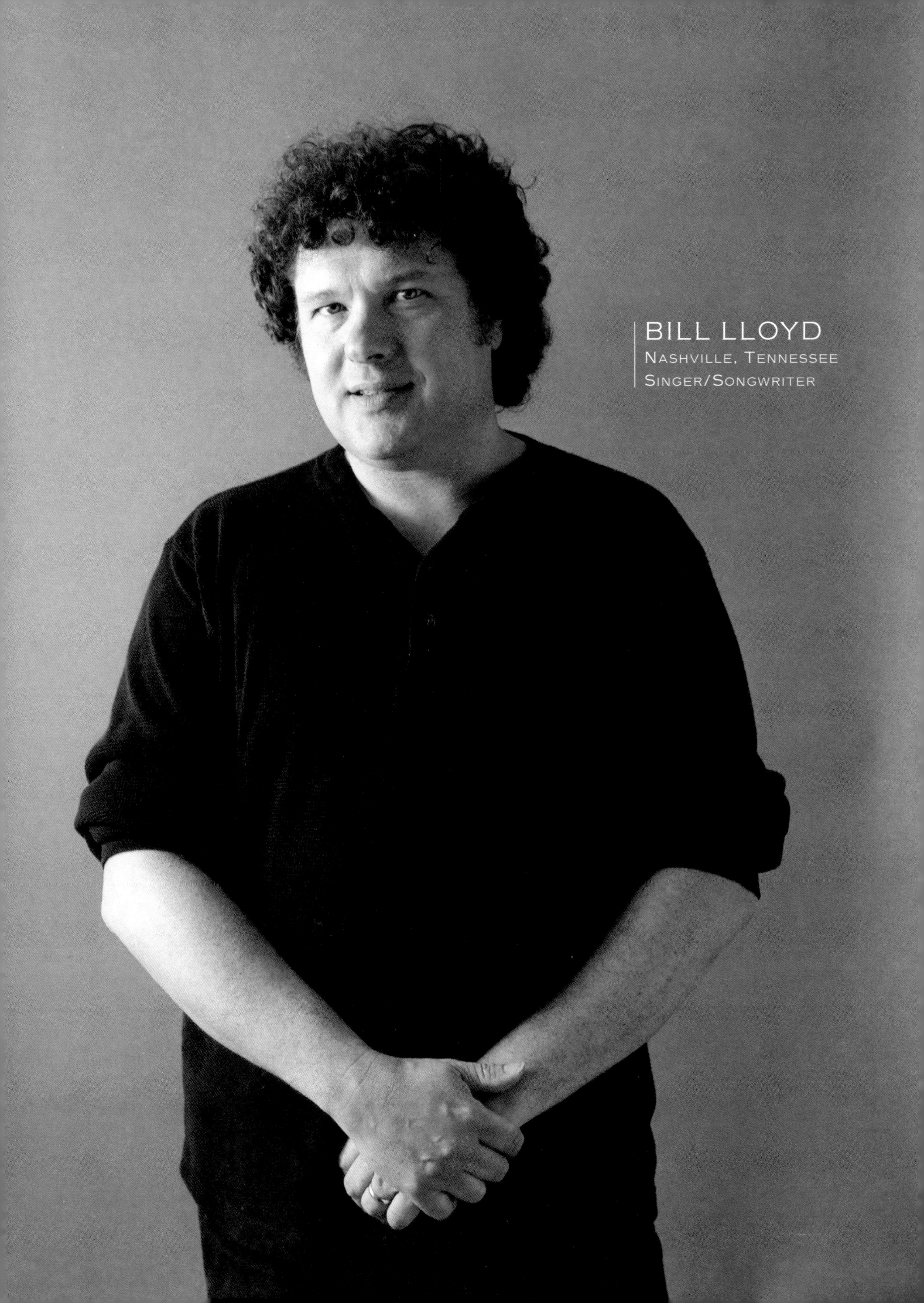

BILL LLOYD
Nashville, Tennessee
Singer/Songwriter

THE INDUSTRY OF DREAMS *For everyone who makes it in the music industry, there are many who never will. But don't be tricked into thinking that anyone ever succeeded without the support of others. That isn't to say that there has never been a pilgrim in our midst who hasn't at times felt completely alone in their quest. But, if truth be told, for Nashville to be a town of dreamers it must by necessity be a town of dream-makers, too. These are the people who give direction and meaning to the dreams of others. More often than not, they are the ones who keep the dreamers on course and breathe life into their hopes and desires.*

Like the dreamers themselves, the dream-makers migrate to Nashville from coast-to-coast. Many among their ranks came with the purpose of working in the music industry, although some of the most successful among them are men and women who arrived as artists and songwriters themselves. Whatever their original intent, it's the music publishers and producers, A & R people and club owners, publicists, and record moguls; individuals from every level of this corporate world, from the tape- and mail rooms to the executive suites, who are in the business of making musicians' dreams come true.

OPPOSITE
DANIEL HILL
OAK RIDGE, TENNESSEE
MUSIC PUBLISHER/WANNABE GUITARIST

ABOVE
LINDA EDELL
THE JERSEY SHORE
ENTERTAINMENT LAWYER
DOUG HOWARD
BOOT HEEL OF MISSOURI
SENIOR V.P. OF A & R

RIGHT
AL BUNETTA
GARFIELD, NEW JERSEY
ARTIST MANAGER/RECORD MOGUL

TONY BROWN
WINSTON-SALEM, NORTH CAROLINA
PIANO PLAYER/PRODUCER/RECORD MOGUL

TIM DuBOIS
GROVE, OKLAHOMA
SONGWRITER/RECORD MOGUL

When Tim DuBois and Tony Brown sit down together at Elliston Soda Shop the balance of power within Nashville's entire music industry begins to shift.

Michel had hoped that the two of them would be willing to be photographed together because both started out as dreamers. They both endorsed the concept without hesitation. Michel had told me nightmarish stories of photographing other captains of power in the past when the games of one-upmanship had become near deadly, so I was understandably uneasy. In fact, photographing Tony and Tim went so smoothly the shoot was finished within minutes. They hardly had time to finish their sodas.

Tim asked us not to let his office know that the shoot had ended so quickly, as he wanted to take the rest of the afternoon off. This was the same Tim DuBois who came to Nashville from Oklahoma by way of Texas as the songwriter of "She Got the Gold Mine, I Got The Shaft," "When I Call Your Name," "Bluest Eyes In Texas," and "Love In The First Degree." Add to these achievements his jobs as C.P.A., artist manager, business school professor. Under his leadership, Arista-Nashville has become a powerhouse of a record company guiding the careers of Alan Jackson, Brooks and Dunn, Pam Tillis, and a host of others over the years.

Tony Brown grew up in the Piedmont area of North Carolina. His dad was a preacher and the family made up a gospel act. They traveled from church to church in a car that had a sign on the back end that admonished one and all to "Trust Jesus."

Tony did and eventually he was playing piano for J.D. Sumner and The Stamps Quartet. This would lead him into Elvis's personal gospel band, "The Voice." After the King had left the building, Tony moved on to other bands, including Emmylou Harris' before he found his calling as ace producer and head of MCA Records with artists like George Strait, Reba McEntire, Vince Gill, and Trisha Yearwood.

So Alex saw me in a bar one night and said he wanted to be photographed by Michel for our book. He pointed out that, like Nashville, this book was probably going to be way too white. As a Mexican-Texan, he was an "angle" that we needed and, if I agreed, he wanted to be photographed in full mariachi costume.

Several days later he called and said he couldn't find a mariachi outfit, so would a matador do? When he finally showed up for the shoot, Alex looked like an extra from a bad coffee commercial. So much for the mariachi and the matador.

Truth is, we would have taken his picture without the costume. Then again, it was way too amusing watching Alex angle his way in to the book to have told him that.

You see, while Alex came to Nashville from Floydada, Texas, as a drummer and musician, his real gift is angling. Publisher, promoter, song-plugger, career-developer — Alex works it hard all the time, yet somehow it's never offensive. You know you are being "angled," whether it's to cut his song, sign his artist, or back his latest scheme. Somehow, you end up liking him all the more.

Kevin Welch once told me that the best folks in the world are in our business. Maybe he was thinking of Alex: drummer, publisher, manager, dreamer, angler — rotten accessorizer.

JOZEF NUYENS
Antwerp, Belgium
Producer/
Music Publisher/
Studio Owner

THE ROUND *Second only to the Opry in its heyday, Amy Kurland's Bluebird Cafe serves as a magnet to all who come with dreams to Nashville. Under her guidance the club has played an influential and celebrated role in the shaping of contemporary country music. Every songwriter who has shown up in town over the last decade or so has made his way to the Bluebird. For no matter where they come from, they all know the stories that surround this revered bar in a strip mall on Hillsboro Road.*

Yet unlike her legendary predecessors Tootsie Best and Miss Wanda of Tootsie's Orchid Lounge, Amy Kurland has built neither her fame nor the renown of the Bluebird by playing the part of the good-hearted barmaid. You don't show up at the Bluebird to unload your woes on Amy. Even if she did work behind the bar, the whines of the down-and-out would be quickly shushed.

For first and foremost, the Bluebird is a performance stage for songwriters. Whether an artist is performing in a traditional style on stage, or seated in the center of the room facing three to five other songwriters in a "round," the songwriter and his craft reign here.

Amy's rounds at the Bluebird are filled with the stuff dreams are made of. Whether she invented the round or not, she has taken it to a plane above all the rest. Although Nashville now has many clubs using the same format, it's the stories of these discoveries that keeps the Bluebird crowded. In providing this place where songs could be heard, Amy has played an important role in launching the careers of many a Nashville artist.

LEFT
PAUL BRANDT
CALGARY, ALBERTA
SINGER/SONGWRITER

ABOVE
SKIP EWING
MILITARY BASES EVERYWHERE
SINGER/SONGWRITER

RIGHT
BRYAN WHITE
LAWTON, OKLAHOMA
SINGER/SONGWRITER/PRODUCER

AMY KURLAND
NASHVILLE, TENNESSEE
OWNER OF THE BLUEBIRD CAFE

HAZEL SMITH
CASWELL COUNTY, NORTH CAROLINA
WRITER/PUBLICIST/CHEERLEADER/CONFIDANTE

The legendary country music publicist and journalist Hazel Smith claims she has done everything but hook to make a living and now regrets that she didn't at least try the ancient trade. Whether reminiscing about a dear friend who has gone to Heaven to be with Jesus, or fantasizing about running over one of her enemies and getting off scott-free "because of her bad eye," Hazel Smith remains the real thing.

She came to Nashville from Caswell County, North Carolina, two sons in tow, with all her worldly possessions in the back of a pickup truck. That first year was spent doing whatever she could to feed her family. Eventually the door of the music industry cracked wide enough for her to slip through.

During the course of her career, Hazel has written for fan magazines, scripted industry newsletters, and created her own syndicated radio show. She has worked as manager, personal assistant, and director of operations for artists as diverse as Dr. Hook, Ricky Skaggs, and Bill Monroe. Hazel coined the phrase "outlaw music" to describe the work of Willie, Waylon, and Kris.

But her real power in Nashville lies in her ability to be a friend, cheerleader, confidante, ally, and counselor to many a young musician when they need one. Her credibility rests on her sincere belief in the power of country music. Every time she hears Alan Jackson sing Gene Watson's "Farewell Party," Hazel is brought to tears. While she remains one of Nashville's best storytellers, Hazel has always shot straight when someone needed to hear the truth. She may be the closest thing country music ever has to Madame Récamier.

LEGENDS

Their stories have been told and retold—for these are the legends of Guitar Town. While every story is unique, they are connected by a common thread spun from talent, perseverance, and luck. Over years filled with both struggle and success, some of them have become friends, some even family, yet each has made his or her own journey, finding the right path to arrive here.

It is often easier for those at a distance to recognize when a pilgrim crosses that magical border to become a legend, than it is for the pilgrim to realize his own arrival. Some arrived as hillbillies, others by way of rock 'n roll, bluegrass, or folk, yet all have overcome the odds against success.

Their stories are not our only stories, but they are the ones we focus on. They are the beacon light that draws us toward that golden border.

Beth Nielson Chapman woke me early one Saturday morning with her call. She wanted to know if Michel still wanted to photograph Chet Atkins. If so, we needed to meet at the Cracker Barrel within an hour. Michel had planned to photograph Chet on a previous visit but a conflict of schedules had made it impossible.

By the time he left high school, Chet Atkins was a proficient guitarist. By age twenty-two, he was playing with Red Foley on the Opry, but because the arrangements Chet heard in his head weren't what the radio executives wanted, he kept getting fired. The day before his wedding, he was fired for the eighth time.

In 1955, Chet scored his first instrumental hit, "Mr. Sandman." When RCA's Steve Scholes was made head of pop A & R in New York, he made his old friend head of RCA/Nashville. This may have been one of the first times an inmate had been given charge over an asylum. Under his leadership the company flourished.

Chet signed Bobby Bare, Waylon Jennings, Don Gibson, Charley Pride, Connie Smith, Floyd Cramer and a host of other notables. He arranged Elvis's first Nashville sessions and played guitar on "Heartbreak Hotel." Dreamer. Dreammaker. Legend.

Of course, Chet was critical to this project. Within thirty minutes we were packed and on our way to the Cracker Barrel. Hearty breakfast, reasonable prices, Chet Atkins on the guitar — who could ask for anything more?

Harriet Tyne is a child of Old Nashville. Now she finds herself somewhat of a grande dame of the same. That was never her ambition in life, but it happens when you're in your ninth decade, in comfortable circumstances, with lots of stories, and you don't seem to be going anywhere soon.

She can vividly recall her childhood growing up in one of the big townhouses that once surrounded the capitol in downtown Nashville. She can recall when her grandparents moved out West End to what is now Montgomery Bell Academy, and when her parents built what later became Ensworth School.

Harriet seems able to remember every party anyone of her set ever gave—and in those days there were lots of parties in Nashville. An exception to this rule of the rulers of Nashville were the Cheeks of Cheekwood. Harriet says they gave only seven parties in the quarter of a century they lived there. Seven parties in twenty-five years was not a good track record in Nashville. She can't ever remember the Cheeks letting anyone use their bathrooms at any of their seven parties. They always rented port-a-lets for their guests. According to Harriet, it was only after Huldah Cheek Sharp gave her family home to Nashville to become a fine arts center and botanical gardens that their friends finally got a good flush there.

The first party at Cheekwood was the B.C. party. Everyone had to come as someone before Christ. Harriet dyed her hair flaming red. When her mother asked who on earth she was going as, Harriet replied, "A vestal virgin," and then asked, "Do you think I'll pass?" "Don't worry," her mother assured her, "Nashville hasn't seen a virgin in years; no one will ever know the difference."

She says that back then no matter where you went, whether to New York, New Orleans, Boston, or Palm Beach, everyone who was anyone knew that Nashville was the best party town in America. She then asks, "When did the best party town in America become Music City, U.S.A.? I think it's somewhat of a comedown, if you get my drift."

HARRIET TYNE
NASHVILLE, TENNESSEE
GRANDE DAME

EARL SCRUGGS

CLEVELAND COUNTY, NORTH CAROLINA
THREE-FINGER STYLE BANJO VIRTUOSO/
SONGWITER/MEMBER,
COUNTRY MUSIC HALL OF FAME

In 1945, bluegrass music jumped a light-year or two in its development when a twenty-one year old North Carolina boy named Earl Scruggs played his three-finger roll for Bill Monroe backstage at the Grand Ole Opry. *Monroe hired him on the spot and Earl found himself traveling around the country with the Bluegrass Boys. Included in the band was fellow player Lester Flatt.*

Three years later, Earl and Lester quit Monroe's band and formed Flatt and Scruggs, conceivably country music's most famous bluegrass band. In the late 1960s, Flatt and Scruggs hit the big time: first with the chart-topping theme song of The Beverly Hillbillies, *"The Ballad of Jed Clampett," and then with Earl's composition "Foggy Mountain Breakdown" when it became the theme song for the movie* Bonnie and Clyde.

By 1969, the duo had split and Earl formed the Earl Scruggs Review with his sons Randy, Gary, and Steve. A whole new generation was introduced to traditional country and bluegrass music when they joined The Nitty Gritty Dirt Band's watershed production Will The Circle Be Unbroken *along with the likes of Mother Maybelle Carter, Jimmy Martin, Merle Travis, and Doc Watson.*

Now off the road, Earl and his wife/business manager, Louise, spend their days surrounded by their children and grandchildren, all trying not to get lost in one of Nashville's landmark monuments to country music; George Jones and Tammy Wynette's 1960s manse, "First Lady Acres."

FAIRFIELD FOUR

FROM LEFT
ROBERT HAMLETT
ISAAC FREEMAN
JAMES HILL
NASHVILLE, TENNESSEE
GOSPEL SINGERS

The morning we arrived to photograph Fairfield Four, which is normally five, we had three. Wilson Water and Joseph Rice couldn't get away from their day jobs at a local golf course. We assumed we would reschedule the shoot but the guys explained that the odds of getting everyone together were rather slim. Besides, the number—which has gone up and down over the years—never has meant much to the Fairfield Four.

In the 1940s, when this group was known nationwide through their daily 6:45 A.M. live performance on WLAC radio's Sunway Vitamin Company Show, one or another of Fairfield Four often slept in. On more than one occasion only Sam McCrary and James Hill made it to the broadcast; on those days the show's white announcer, Herman Grizzard, was drafted to provide the missing harmony. Sure enough, it always seemed that folks would go out of their way to compliment those particular performances unaware of Herman's contribution.

So, with three of the five called four in tow, we went ahead with the shoot. Unfortunately, Herman Grizzard isn't around to fill in anymore.

RAY PRICE
Perryville, Texas
Country Crooner/
Member, Country Music
Hall of Fame

PETER FRAMPTON
BECKENHAM, ENGLAND
GUITARIST/SONGWRITER/SINGER

GUY CLARK
MONAHANS, TEXAS
TROUBADOUR
SUSANNE CLARK
ATLANTA, TEXAS
PAINTER/SONGWRITER

A blue blood among Texas troubadours, Guy Clark has probably forgotten more songs that he's crafted than most songwriters ever write.

Add to this prodigiousness his partnership with Susanne, both a painter and a songwriter, and you've got a lot of energy concentrated in one place on earth.

OPPOSITE

RIDLEY WILLS II
NASHVILLE, TENNESSEE
HISTORIAN/AUTHOR/
POSTCARD COLLECTOR/
PRESERVATIONIST
IRENE WILLS
NASHVILLE, TENNESSEE
PRESERVATIONIST

ABOVE

SAM FLEMING
NASHVILLE, TENNESSEE &
PALM BEACH, FLORIDA
BANKER/BUSINESS LEADER/
COMMUNITY PHILANTHROPIST
VALERIE FLEMING
NASHVILLE, TENNESSEE &
PALM BEACH, FLORIDA
COMMUNITY PHILANTHROPIST

NAOMI JUDD
ASHLAND, KENTUCKY
ARTIST/SONGWRITER/
AUTHOR/MOTHER

If there is a Queen Mother of country music today it must surely be Naomi Judd.

She first came to Nashville in 1979 with her daughters Wynonna and Ashley. She supported them by working as a nurse while she worked Music Row with an undaunted zeal.

It was in a hospital and not a record company that Naomi met her future producer Brent Maher. The Judds' first single was released by 1983. Between then and when Naomi left the road because of chronic hepatitis, the Judds became one of the most successful female acts in country music history.

While Wynonna went on with her music career and her younger sister Ashley became an actress, their mother seemed content to write and lecture in retirement. But with her recovery, Naomi has begun to reinvent her life again, this time with the additional role of counselor and motivator.

When Michel showed up to photograph Naomi, it was clear from the first that he was no longer in charge. With the same inner strength that has been the signature of her life and music, Naomi gently guided all of us through the shoot, offering insights into healthier living along the way. Being both a man who loves strong women and someone who has spent at least a bit of his life photographing royals, Michel almost instantly felt at ease within her court.

It was only after he returned to his photo lab in New York that Michel realized that the sultry photographs were more evocative of Cecil Beaton's images of the young Elizabeth II of the 1950s than they were to hillbilly royalty. By her own willpower and determination to transform herself, Naomi Judd has surely earned a royal title.

CHARLIE DANIELS
WILMINGTON, NORTH CAROLINA
SINGER/ARTIST/FIDDLER/SONGWRITER

HARLAN HOWARD

DETROIT, MICHIGAN
SONGWRITER/MEMBER,
COUNTRY MUSIC HALL OF FAME

Harlan Howard likes to tell the story of how Hank Cochran brought him the beginning of "I Fall to Pieces." In a dazzling burst of creativity, they finished writing the song within minutes. What they had just written would become one of Patsy Cline's biggest hits. The only problem was Patsy didn't like it. Her career was in a slump, and she needed a hit, but she was sure that "I Fall to Pieces" would bury any chance she had.

Patsy finally gave in and "I Fall to Pieces" turned her career around. It led to a string of hits that made her one of the top recording artists in the country at the time of her death in 1963.

Harlan is full of stories from a life well lived. He has written hits for generations and has known everyone along the way. His friends and comrades pass away over the years, and periodically he moves on to a new bar, but the hits and stories never seem to end.

BILLY COX
WHEELING, WEST VIRGINIA
BASS PLAYER

Billy Cox first met Jimi Hendrix when they were both stationed in an army camp north of Nashville in the early 1960s. From the very start, music was the bond of a lifetime friendship. Little did either of them know when they formed a band how far music would take them or how short Jimi's lifetime would be.

After serving their time in the army, Billy came to Nashville while Jimi ended up in New York City. One night Jimi called Billy and told him that some white guys in New York wanted him to do an album. Jimi wanted to start a new band and wanted Billy to join him. Billy asked just how he was supposed to come up with the money to get to New York. Jimi said he would get a job and earn the money Billy needed for the bus ticket. Several weeks later Jimi called back to say he had earned the money.

Billy took the bus that next day and once he arrived in New York things never slowed down. After Jimi's death in 1970, Billy continued to play their

old haunts. Eventually, he ended up back in Nashville. Today he works in a pawn shop off Murfreesboro Road.

His guitar playing and its impact on music, along with his witness to those times, has made the pawn shop a shrine for music historians try-ing to chronicle the past and young guitarists trying to recreate it.

LITTLE JIMMY DICKENS

Raleigh County, West Virginia
Member, Grand Ole Opry/
Member, Country Music Hall of Fame

JOHN HIATT
INDIANAPOLIS, INDIANA
ARTIST/SONGWRITER

NANCY STANLEY HIATT
NASHVILLE, TENNESSEE
HORSE LOVER

In a town known for its singer-songwriters, John Hiatt stands in the company of a handful at the top of the heap. Praised by the critics, revered by his peers, John writes about his life, his amazing wife Nancy, and their kids—the ups and downs of daily existence at the end of one century and the beginning of another.

His songs tell the story of someone a bit uncomfortable with becoming too comfortable with his life. Far from the formulaic mid-tempo love songs that seem to be the scourge of contemporary Nashville songwriting, John offers us glimpses of a life filled with both love and fear, doubt and lust, and above all, humor. They seem to be the reflections of someone who spent too many years taking life way too seriously to take that path again.

A son of Indiana, John has lived and worked in both Nashville and Los Angeles, but in the end, Nashville seemed to fit him best.

PORTER WAGONER
West Plains, Missouri
Member, Grand Ole Opry

LARRY CARLTON
Los Angeles, California
Guitarist
MICHELE PILLAR CARLTON
Westminster, California
Recording Artist

Unlike so many transplants from southern California, Larry Carlton arrived neither looking for work nor fleeing his past. He first came to Nashville to be near his children.

As a world-class guitarist, Larry can and does work everywhere. It's as easy for him to be based on a small farm near Leiper's Fork, Tennessee, as it is to be based in Los Angeles.

Larry handles the changes and shifts of life with the same signature grace for which his guitar-playing is legendary. What's the big deal about pulling up lifetime roots and moving your wife, her horse, and your guitars across the United States? Really not much at all, after surviving a violent crime that left him about as close to dead as it comes without an obituary. And when he did survive the life or death issue, then came the pronouncement that he would never play again and, with it, his long struggle to prove that one wrong, too.

Despite all the curves in the road Larry seems to be living a life full of grace. He seems as excited about a good cheeseburger at Pucket's Grocery as he is about an upcoming album. As he lay in a hospital bed and reviewed all that had come before, he concluded that somehow now it would all be good.

His dream was born on the front porch of his grandmother's house in Oklahoma as the family sat around and played and sang. From the very beginning he wanted nothing more than to play the guitar. His mother refused to let him start lessons until he could at least hold the guitar by himself. Larry sometimes wonders what he could have done with his life if only he could have started earlier. Then again he concludes—it really doesn't matter, it's all good anyway.

MAURA O'CONNELL
ENNIS, COUNTY CLARE, IRELAND
SINGER

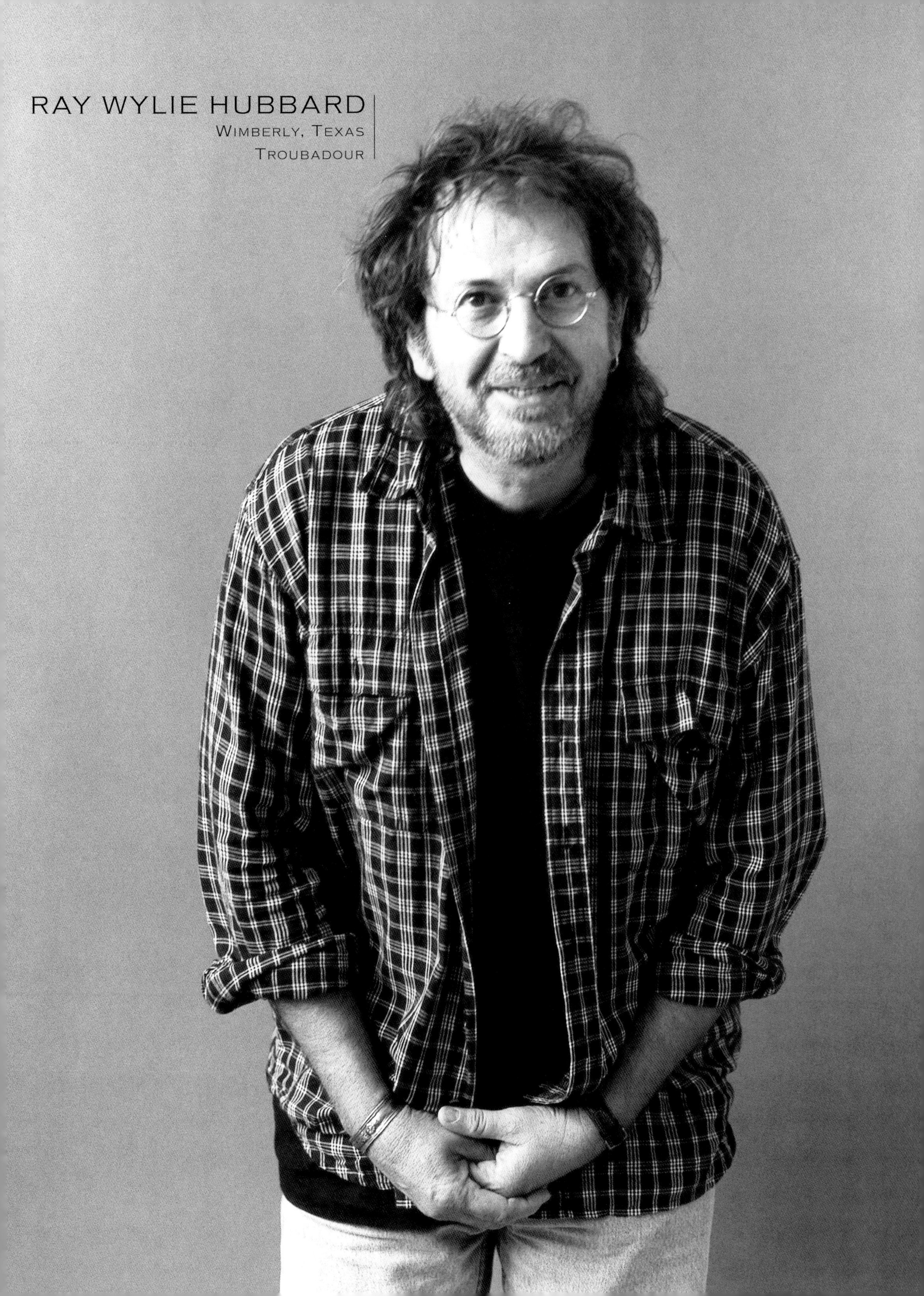

RAY WYLIE HUBBARD
Wimberly, Texas
Troubadour

ALAN JACKSON
NEWNAN, GEORGIA
ARTIST/SONGWRITER/MEMBER,
GRAND OLE OPRY

Neither Michel nor I ever envisioned this book as another homage to the stars of country music. That book has already been published in multiple forms to varying degrees of success over the years. We hoped to portray dreamers, whether street musicians or Opry stars, not necessarily success stories.

That said, from almost that first night in that bar on Lower Broadway, Michel wanted to photograph Alan Jackson. If anyone was to be included in the circle of those who have made it, Alan needed to be there. For Alan is, as Michel has often insisted, "the real deal." In the tradition of both singer and songwriter, Alan has built a career by telling his own story, his own way. The child of a family of modest circumstances, but rich in values, his songs often give us glimpses into both the simplicity and depth of this heritage. He sings candidly of his shortcomings and his struggles to do right and make sense of this life. The complexity of this heritage is with him still. When we arrived at his farm outside of Nashville we found Alan and his family surrounded by all the trappings of his success. From his car collection to the state-of-the-art electronics to the minute detailing of the house, offices, cabin, barns, pools, ponds, and airfield, everything gives witness to the rewards of the awards that line the library walls. Yet in the midst of all they have, we found both Alan and his wife Denise working at the job of being parents, trying to ground themselves and hold on to the family here in the real world.

JOHN KAY

EAST PRUSSIA, GERMANY
& LOS ANGELES, CALIFORNIA
FOUNDING MEMBER &
LEAD SINGER, STEPPENWOLF

DICKEY LEE
MEMPHIS, TENNESSEE
SONGWRITER/ARTIST

DELBERT McCLINTON
FORT WORTH, TEXAS
ARTIST/SONGWRITER

BUDDY MILLER
FAIRBORN, OHIO
SINGER/SONGWRITER

JULIE MILLER
AUSTIN, TEXAS
GUITAR PLAYER/ARTIST/PRODUCER

Like many a musician, Buddy has taken a long road to Nashville. His career started out in upstate New York. Along the way, Buddy lived in San Francisco, Seattle, New York City, Austin, and Los Angeles before settling down in Nashville with his musical partner, Julie.

Julie's early years were spent in Waxahachie, Texas. When she was seven her family moved to Austin.

It was in Austin that Buddy met Julie when they got together in a band where she was the girl singer.

Buddy's ground-breaking record, Your Love and Other Lies *with five cowrites and two solo compositions by Julie, was called "the country album of the decade" by Steve Earle. Add to this Julie's beautifully crafted albums* Blue Pony *and* Broken Things, *their individual and partnered compositions for a wide range of country and Americana artists, and Buddy's continuing work with Emmylou Harris and Jim Lauderdale. Producer, band leader, sideman, songwriter, he seems to have his bases covered.*

When we arrived to photograph Buddy and Julie, the whole setting lent itself to a rather formal Edwardian portrait. Here were two of Nashville's more successful left-of-center singer-songwriters in a very controlled image. Controlled that was, until Julie opened up the can of tuna fish.

DOLLY PARTON

SEVIER COUNTY, TENNESSEE
ICON/MEMBER, GRAND OLE OPRY/
MOVIE STAR/MEMBER,
COUNTRY MUSIC HALL OF FAME

In country music, Dolly's story is every woman's story, no matter where she comes from or what her circumstances. At least that's what we would like to believe.

She was born in poverty in Sevier County in the mountains of East Tennessee—one of twelve children. As a child she used her ability to make up songs and sing them as a way to both escape and celebrate her humble surroundings. By the age of ten, Dolly was performing regularly on the Cas Walker TV show in Knoxville.

In high school she told her friends that after graduation she was going to Nashville to become a star. When she became the first member of her family to graduate from high school, Dolly bought a bus ticket for Nashville. Sure enough, three years later she joined Porter Wagoner and was featured on his weekly syndicated TV show.

The partnership ended rather badly when Dolly wanted to move on. After a very public split, Dolly wrote "I Will Always Love You" for Porter, but he never saw a cent of the publishing. It remains one of the all-time best selling songs. It has been a number one hit twice for Dolly on the country charts, a worldwide pop hit for Whitney Houston, and again a hit, this time as a duet for Dolly and Vince Gill.

In the years that followed, Dolly went on not only to record her own music, but to act in films, open an amusement park at her childhood home, and build a personal fortune. She has created an image that has become an American icon. Although she spends less time in Nashville these days, she remains the very symbol of this city and of all our dreams come true.

JAY McINERNEY
New York, New York
Author
HELEN BRANSFORD McINERNEY
Nashville, Tennessee
Author/Pig Farmer/Jewelry Designer

HUNTER KAY

PALESTINE, TEXAS
AUTHOR/GARDENER/
COLLECTOR/ANTIQUE DEALER

Hunter Kay came to Nashville from Palestine, Texas to go to Vanderbilt. He describes his parents as a marriage of Imelda Marcos and Mahatma Gandhi.

He doesn't play guitar. For years when his speakers were shot some questioned whether he could even play a stereo. "Something in Red" is his favorite country song this side of Patsy Cline. Most of us maintain that "Something in Red" is not a country song. Hunter says maybe that's why it's his favorite country song. No one ever asks Hunter's opinion about country music. But then again, he has rarely ever waited for an invitation to express his opinion on anything.

After graduation from college and after a brief stint working in the oil fields of Louisiana, Hunter returned to Nashville. He began to build a house in the woods south of the city. He had no real practical experience, although he did read a book on building. He built his house without running water or electricity. The only electrified object he had was the stereo with the shot speakers, which he would hook up to his truck battery. You always knew when Hunter had a great party and didn't invite you, because he would call you up the next morning and ask you to give him a jump.

Hunter wrote what the late southern novelist and critic Andrew Lytle called "the finest short story written in the second half of the twentieth century." It's included in most anthologies of modern southern literature.

Hunter is a gardener and a collector of objects depicting the Sacred Heart of Jesus. He commissioned a pyramid to be built in his garden out of angle iron after seeing the pyramid-tomb Caius Cestius built in Rome. A reluctant creature of our age, Hunter remains a pilgrim in search of a world which may never have been.

JULES SHEAR
BEARSVILLE, NEW YORK
ARTIST/SONGWRITER/PRODUCER

9 M   1/30   F 5.6 ±0.0Ev   75 mm

LEON RUSSELL
Tulsa, Oklahoma
Rock Star

LAMAR SORRENTO
MEMPHIS, TENNESSEE
OUTSIDER ARTIST/SONGWRITER/
RECORDING ARTIST/GUITAR TRADER

*Lamar Sorrento doesn't live in Nashville.
He lives in Memphis, which is three hours
and many mind-sets away from Nashville.
Memphis was developed and laid out by the
movers and shakers of nineteenth century
Nashville. That's pretty much when we
parted ways. Memphis is delta blues;
Nashville is hillbilly.*

*Lamar's real name is James Eddie
Campbell. For a long time he called himself
"the other Eddie" so as not to be confused
with guitar great Eddie Lang. Eddie Lang is
Lamar's, that is James Eddie's, that is "the
other Eddie's," greatest hero. Well, actually
not his greatest hero: that, of course, would*
be Django Reinhardt. In any case, Eddie Lang is way up there in Lamar's book.

*Lamar is a guitarist, songwriter, and recording artist. When he's not pursuing
these trades, Lamar is buying and selling guitars. When all else fails, Lamar is a
painter. He rarely portrays anyone who is not a musician. Favorite musicians like
Django, Eddie, the Beatles, and Hank Williams have been painted again and again.*

*Sometimes Lamar breaks the barrier that separates Memphis from Nashville.
Most often he comes to Nashville for guitar shows, or to an opening of his work.
Then again he may show up at a guitar pull or to play a club date. He will never
fit into anyone's image of Nashville, nor will his music. Yet, over the years he has
built a small loyal following of friends and fellow musicians in Guitar Town.
He gives a deeper understanding to the title "Outside Artist."*

SANDY BULL
New York, New York
Guitarist/Songwriter

CONNIE SMITH
ELKHART, INDIANA
COUNTRY MUSIC QUEEN/
MEMBER, GRAND OLE OPRY
MARTY STUART
PHILADELPHIA, MISSISSIPPI
MEMBER, GRAND OLE OPRY/SINGER/
PHOTOGRAPHER/COLLECTOR

JIM HORN
<small>LOS ANGELES, CALIFORNIA
HORN PLAYER</small>

In a town of guitar players, Jim Horn remains a sideman. As sidemen go, Jim is among the best in the world. He has worked with everyone from Eric Clapton and the Beatles to Garth Brooks and John Denver. His famous sensitivity of style, on everything from the saxophone to the recorder, has made Jim a consummate studio musician and stage sideman.

Because of his catholic tastes in music, Jim has settled comfortably into the world of hillbilly music, in the hills of Tennessee.

STONEWALL JACKSON
<small>(RIGHT) WITH THE MINUTEMEN
TABOR CITY, NORTH CAROLINA
MEMBER, GRAND OLE OPRY</small>

BILLY RAY CYRUS
FLATWOODS, KENTUCKY
SINGER/SONGWRITER

*From the very beginning of this project, Michel
and I knew that we could not possibly tell the
story of Guitar Town without Billy Ray Cyrus.
After all, his pilgrimage parallels the story of so
many others who have come to Nashville seeking
fame and fortune. However, this parallel ended
when the song "Achy Breaky Heart," off Billy's
first album, took him on a meteoric journey that
few have ever traveled. Overnight, Billy was
thrust into the national spotlight.*

*What made it worse to his detractors was
that Billy seemed to savor it all. He understood
his fans' love of the song and of him.*

*In going further than anyone had gone
before, with a song the industry hated, Billy Ray
Cyrus sealed his fate in the eyes of many.
Dismissed by his peers for the crime of riding the
wave, he's a legend, but will remain forever a
pilgrim. In the end, maybe that's the best award
Nashville could give him.*

INDEX OF PORTRAITS